Guidebooks for Counsellors

Counsellors in the course of their practice ar
particular difficulties, such as experience of incest, drug or alcohol addiction, or eating difficulties. These issues may not be the main focus of the counselling and it may not be appropriate to refer the client on to a specialist in one of these fields, if such exists locally. There may be literature available but little guidance for the counsellor seeking it.

The Publications Sub-Committee of the British Association for Counselling are publishing a series of booklets to help counsellors in this situation. Written by specialist counsellors or therapists, they draw attention to issues which are likely to arise for the client and for the counsellor and which may be missed by the novice. They also provide a guide to the relevant literature. Being brief, readable and to the point it is hoped that counsellors will be able to consult them even when time and money are short. In this way it is hoped that these booklets will contribute to the raising of standards of counselling in general.

The Sub-Committee would like to thank not only those members who worked to produce these booklets, but also Isobel Palmer and Sally Cook, and the consultant editors, myself, Gladeana McMahon and Stephen Palmer, whose contribution was vital.

Julia Segal
Chair, Publications Sub-Committee of the
British Association for Counselling.

Carole Waskett

After an interesting but complicated life up to the age of 33, Carole had her first and only child, divorced, and went to University. Since then she has completed

a further degree course, worked as a Samaritan and a co-counsellor, become a workshop leader at the Women's Therapy Centre, and developed a long-standing private counselling and training practice, specialising in working with people in eating distress. For the last four years she has also worked for East Suffolk MIND and spends a day each week as a counsellor in primary care. She lives with her son and three cats in Ipswich.

Counselling People

in Eating Distress

Carole Waskett

Learning Resources Centre

British Association for Counselling
1 Regent Place • Rugby • Warwickshire CV21 2PJ
Office 01788 550899 • Information Line 01788 578328 • Fax 01788 562189

© **BAC 1993   ISBN   0 946181 39 X**

Published by the British Association for Counselling, 1 Regent Place, Rugby, Warwickshire CV21 2PJ

First printed 1993

Produced by   BAC, company limited by guarantee 2175320 and
                   registered charity 298361
Printed by   Quorn Litho, Queens Road, Loughborough,
                   Leicestershire LE11 1HH

Others in the series:

Counselling Adults who were Abused as Children
Counselling People with Infertility Problems

British Association for Counselling

- Codes of Ethics & Practice for Counsellors, for Counselling Skills, for Trainers, for the Supervision of Counsellors
- Counselling publications mail order service
- Quarterly journal with in-depth articles, news and views of members
- Individual Accreditation, Supervisor Recognition and Counsellor Course Recognition schemes

Join BAC now - the Voice of Counselling

Details of the above and much more besides:
BAC, 1 Regent Place, Rugby CV21 2PJ.
Tel: 01788 550899

Foreword

Over the period of a year, Eating Disorders Association (EDA) receives a large number of enquiries from counsellors wanting advice on how to help someone in eating distress, lists of courses available, or more commonly, asking if we know of an 'expert' in the area to whom a client may be referred.

For many counsellors, eating disorder clients have a reputation for being hard to help, being 'manipulative and difficult'. Carole Waskett's new guide book throws a welcome and refreshingly different light on this perception of people with eating disorders, and her enthusiasm is infectious. She finds them 'stressful, intriguing, absorbing and a delight', and her book challenges other counsellors to welcome and enjoy working with them too.

Carole's vivid case studies bring life to the sort of feelings and pressures experienced by women in eating distress, and help the reader to get inside their world. Her careful analysis of the important features to remember in counselling form a valuable and down to earth guide - points like; valuing the eating behaviour of a client as a necessary way for her to express her feelings, rather than a nuisance to be eradicated quickly - understanding the metaphors of eating behaviour and using them.

There is advice on many practical issues which may worry a counsellor - for example, how to ensure the safety of your client and interacting with a GP when necessary.

The thread running through this guide is sensitivity, care, respect and understanding for your client, and we at EDA would recommend it most highly. We hope it may encourage more counsellors to have confidence in working in this challenging field, and to welcome clients in eating distress. We feel very hopeful that its use will increase counsellors' confidence and expertise, and will help to ensure in the future a higher standard of readily available care for people with eating disorders.

Ruth O'Beney
Counsellor,
Eating Disorders Association, Norwich

Contents

Introduction

This guidebook is for you if you're interested in counselling people in emotional distress around eating. I'm assuming that you have skills in general counselling, but make no assumptions about your background or orientation. I hope you'll feel encouraged by it, and find it useful.

If you haven't worked with someone in eating distress before, you may feel confused and at sea when your first anorexic, bulimic or compulsively eating client walks in the door. You may have gathered the impression that people with eating disorders are a real problem to work with, manipulative, deceitful and difficult. I'd like to present a different picture. In my experience, working with this particular category of clients is stressful, but it is also intriguing, absorbing, and a delight.

People in eating distress are people just like anyone else in counselling. They are struggling to make sense of and express their feelings about their life. They want to trust you. They want to communicate authentically with you and everyone else in their world. But like most of us, they are afraid. The only difference between them and anyone else is that they have found a syndrome which can be difficult to understand. It is a language, a metaphor, and a solution to the problems in their lives. That syndrome is the eating problem itself.

Eating is the most primitive activity we know. You can be sure that problems around it will be loaded with a tremendous emotional charge. But if your client is willing to come to regular sessions, then together you have a good chance of finding your way across the mysterious dark seas of her experience, towards health. People with these difficulties can and do get better. And if you, her counsellor, are able to stay with her, on her side, it's more than likely that she will find her way towards a more benign and truly nourishing life.

Counselling People in Eating Distress

In general terms there are three forms of emotionally-based eating problem. These are:

Anorexia nervosa

Anorexia nervosa was first reported in 1694 and has been well documented since. Perhaps those Victorian women who 'went into a decline' were anorexic, in unconscious protest against the sweet and passive role it was then fashionable for women to adopt. Because of its dramatic effects, anorexia has had to be taken seriously by the medical and psychiatric professions, and until fairly recently this was the high-profile form of eating disorder, the one into which grant funding and research effort was poured.

Bulimia nervosa

Bulimia nervosa is a much more recently recognised condition, not properly described until the late 1970s. Amongst its characteristics are a strong sense of shame, and thus a need for secrecy; and, often, a body-weight within the normal range. Obviously, these particular characteristics militate against the individual getting help. It therefore seems likely that there are very many more bulimics than come for help. Even so, it's estimated that about 1% of Western females meet the full diagnostic criteria, and a further 2-4% have the sub-clinical syndrome.

Compulsive eating

Compulsive eating as a distinct condition is only recently becoming recognised. It is not included in the official list of psychiatric conditions, nor has it been taken into account in the funding of such bodies as the Eating Disorders Association. However, about 50% of Western women are overweight, on a diet, and/or feel out of control around food. This can cause enormous stress, guilt, stigma, poverty, and social isolation. These are good reasons for accepting compulsive eating as a category of eating distress.

There is no general agreement about the definitions of these forms of distress, and if you are talking with someone about them it's best to clarify exactly what you both mean. For example, many workers ignore compulsive eating altogether or subsume it under bulimia nervosa. Some will just call this 'bulimia'. The word 'bulmarexia' is also in use.

Terminology

The word 'sufferer' is handy but, I believe, a misnomer. It implies that people with eating distress are helpless victims; not an impression I'd want to perpetuate. So in this booklet I use 'person in eating distress' or 'client' instead.

I use the feminine pronoun to refer to the client, not as a sexist assumption but because about 90% of people with eating distress are in fact female. Nevertheless, much of what is said here is also applicable to male clients.

'AEBW' is a term you may see in the literature. It means 'average expected body weight': simply, the weight you might normally expect a person of this sex, age, height and build to be. There are charts to help, but there is no need to start anxiously looking things up. Common sense will tell you and your client what you need to know in most cases, except perhaps if you are working with a very low weight anorexic. Even in this case you can usually tell that your client is physically in jeopardy, and in this situation the client should be seeing her doctor, whose business it is, regularly (see page 26).

'Eating disorders', 'eating problems', or 'eating distress'? All three are used. At a recent conference (October 1991, *Survivors Speak Out*), a majority of people with the problem preferred to call it 'eating distress'. In this booklet I use all three terms, with a leaning towards 'eating distress'.

Seeking help

People in eating distress usually make their GP their first port of call. There, they will probably be given a diet sheet and 'encouragement'. Encouragement to lose weight, eat properly, stop vomiting, and so on. Nowadays, this is still the most commonly met 'treatment'. If the patient fails at this (and after a while, most do) firmer steps are likely to be taken.

In the bad old days, a prescription for an amphetamine-based drug or a stomach-filler might be given to a compulsive eater. Even a bulimic patient might get these if she only told her doctor about the bingeing part of the syndrome. Anorexics and bulimics are often given a prescription for anti-depressants. Perhaps the doctor will ask his patient to record her eating, visit the surgery regularly for weighing, and promise to try really hard to 'control herself'. If this is unsuccessful (and it usually is), the patient might be referred to a dietician or a psychiatrist, or perhaps both.

At this point, often, the patient begins to dodge the surgery guiltily and goes underground, hiding her eating habits from her doctor and from the rest of the world as well. It seems too painful to contemplate giving up the eating behaviour - much as she longs to be free of it. Professionals can become very frustrated. Does she want to get better or doesn't she? The greatest terror is of being made to get 'fat'. If she is a compulsive eater, she fears being put on yet another diet which she can't stick to. It's at this point that these patients begin to get the reputation of being difficult, sly and manipulative. They're not really. They are simply protecting themselves.

But even if the patient does get to the point of being referred on by the GP, she rarely receives any form of psychological counselling. Instead, measures were, and still are, taken which include strict behavioural treatment, administered either as an in-patient or an out-patient. Patients can be kept in hospital, deprived of family, friends, books or TV, or even the 'right' to visit the lavatory, until they put on a certain amount of weight. Stomach stapling or jaw-wiring may be used as a last resort for desperate compulsive eaters. Experimentation with medication continues in an effort to find a drug which will stop people with eating distress from behaving as they do around food.

Cognitive behavioural therapy is a little more attentive to psychological process, in that it works on helping the patient to change the thoughts which are around for her during the eating behaviour. This form of treatment is now much favoured, particularly in the psychiatric world, and some studies have been done from which it is apparent that success rates are quite high, at least in the short term, provided that patients stay the course. There is a variation which includes combined group and individual work, with two-year follow-up after the main treatment of ten sessions.

But in 1978 Susie Orbach published a report of her psychodynamic work with women with eating problems in London in *Fat is a Feminist Issue*. Later, she wrote *Hunger Strike*, about the phenomenon of anorexia nervosa. She was one of many workers who were beginning to understand that eating distress was not the problem, but the *solution*.

Beneath the behaviour was a depth of rich emotional experience longing to be heard. And being ready to listen, in therapy, was a new and productive way to help people presenting with an eating disorder.

When we listen to people talking about their experiences of eating distress, we realise that the fear, anxiety and obsessional feelings around food and weight are a way of communicating inner unhappiness. Maybe, for the time being, there are no other ways to say what has to be said. The whole package - whether it is simply eating too much and feeling fat and depressed, or a highly complex ritualised syndrome comprising eating, vomiting, excessive exercise, social isolation and more - can be seen as a response to social demands and pressures, sadness, anger, frustration or grief.

This understanding means a new way of working with people using the behaviour. It becomes clear that looking at the 'symptoms' as a nuisance to be eradicated, is no more useful than smashing out the malfunction light on a machine, rather than looking inside to see what's wrong.

Nowadays, although many people with eating distress are still offered other types of treatment, more and more are being seen by counsellors and therapists. Counselling is now recognised as a useful and important part of the picture. If you are a counsellor with a chance to work with people in eating distress, go ahead - and enjoy it!

Case Study

Jane is a counsellor in general practice. One of the doctors refers a young woman, Yvette. Yvette tells Jane that for the past three years she has had eating problems. It started when her parents split up soon after her grandmother's death. At the same time Yvette was doing exams at the local FE college.

Since then, Yvette has been in despair about her weight. She began by trying to slim, as she felt fat and disliked at college. She wasn't finding it easy to keep up with the work either. Some time later, she discovered that she could make herself vomit. This meant that she could now give free rein to her desire to fill herself up with delicious food. And then she discovered laxatives. She left college without finishing her course. Now she is in a painful cycle of bingeing, vomiting and laxative abuse.

Despite high aspirations, she has a 'dull'. job in an office, and lives with her mother and sister. Her sister is 'so slim and elegant' and the sisters have a fiercely competitive relationship.

Jane agrees to see Yvette on a weekly basis, and she seems eager to get help. But the next week, she doesn't arrive. The following week there's a problem with transport, but Yvette rushes in twenty minutes late. Jane notices this ambivalence, which happens in various ways over and over again, and brings it to Yvette's attention frequently during their sessions together. At first, Yvette is embarrassed, but later she begins to understand that Jane is simply making the ambivalence conscious so that they can look at it together and try to understand it. Yvette is terrified that Jane will suggest that she stops dieting and bingeing. She is in a surgery, after all, and perhaps she should be making more of an effort, getting better and not 'wasting the counsellor's time'? But eventually she comes to believe that Jane is interested in her inner world, and not in her compliance in 'being good'.

As the weeks roll by, Yvette goes on testing the boundaries in all directions, and when Jane is weary at the end of the day she finds this exasperating. One of the ways Yvette tests her is to ask for guidance on what to eat when. She 'can't remember' what she is supposed to eat, she says, and her appetite doesn't tell her. Yvette is ashamed, but relieved, when she is able to tell Jane exactly how she vomits (by using her toothbrush handle) and how cleansed she feels afterwards.

Many sessions later, Yvette is beginning to sort out how she feels about her parents and her sister, and to grieve for her grandmother's death. In the transference, Jane has stood in for Yvette's grandmother, and later for her sister.

One day Yvette surprises Jane by saying she is going back to college - to do something quite different from what she did before. She needs support for this change. She finds herself bingeing and vomiting more while it happens, and this frightens her. But once her new course starts, she reports that she 'can't be bothered' to binge so much. Her laxative use is dropping rapidly.

Nine months later, Yvette decides to move in with her boyfriend. The relationship seems sound and she is much happier. During the counselling work, Jane has been able to accept Yvette's anger and ambivalence, and helped her to look under the eating behaviour to the distress beneath. At the last session, Yvette says she was very surprised that Jane never encouraged her to stop any of the destructive behaviour. She did it herself, they agree.

Basic Information

At any one time in Britain, one in four people (about 14 million) are 'on a diet'. Many, but not all, of these will be in eating distress of the kind described here. The prevalence of people with specific eating problems is not easily ascertained, because studies are done of particular groups; for example, teenage girls, or students. But most counsellors will come across people in eating distress amongst their clients. Sometimes the eating problem will be the presenting problem; in other cases, the counsellor's alertness to tension or distress around eating may enable the client to begin to disclose behaviour which she has never revealed to anyone else.

There is some basic information which you should know when starting to work with someone in distress about eating. This background information includes understanding the wider perspective, as well as paying sharply focussed attention to the likely realities of the individual's behaviour.

The wider perspective

In the third world, eating distress has an immediate, terrible and different meaning: 'There isn't enough'. Compulsive eating, bulimia and anorexia nervosa are conditions of richer, Western society. Why should it be that people with a choice of plentiful food should develop these distortions of eating behaviour? This question is linked to a further one: why is it mostly (about 90%) *women* in our society who develop eating distress? It is very helpful to the client for you to be aware of the issues that arise from this question.

Over the last twenty years, a great deal of work has been done in this area. The most obvious connection of women with food stems from women as food providers. Women breast feed their children, and, traditionally at least, they are the sex who shop, cook and serve others. The other image that is presented to us is that of the woman who is elegant, sexy and, above all, slim.

The size of a woman's body is important to our society. The ideal is presented in advertising and the media, and public concern about keeping the size of women's bodies in line is expressed by, amongst others, comedians, slimming clubs, and concerned doctors and relatives. Perhaps the size and shape of the body also stands for the size and shape of women's power and influence in what has always been a man's world. The message the world gives to women is 'don't take up too much space'.

So there are two basic archetypes - the bustling earth-mother and the passive, slim sex goddess. These are probably impossible to reconcile, and equally impossible to ignore. A third, more recent cardboard cutout figure is the tough, forthright, unkempt 'women's libber' - yet another image which is too stereotyped to be of use to the majority of women. How many real women's lives have anything to do with these images? And how can real women find models to aim for - role models which encompass the intrinsic qualities women really possess? What's really expected of women, in appearance, behaviour and meaning, and how does this affect their own view of themselves?

If we add to these difficult contradictions the understanding that women are the 'second sex', less powerful than men in society, and that both sexes are now struggling with feminism and its implications, we can see that women in general have to deal with many issues to do with self-image and self-nourishment. The particular client in front of you, while she may not necessarily summarise all these ideas in words, is living in a place and at a time when they are potent in her background and emotional life.

The Individual

What follows is a basic description of the three separate categories of eating distress.

Compulsive eating

Case Study - Ella

Ella is a woman of 48. Her father was in the forces, and the family moved around a good deal when she was a child. Her mother was a quiet, passive woman who was able to offer little protection to her three children when father became drunk and violent. Ella, the oldest child, tried to protect the younger ones, and always felt responsible for them.

As soon as she was old enough, Ella left home. She began a college course, but left after a few months to get married. Her compulsive eating started about now. Her husband became very critical of her increasing weight, and she grew depressed and withdrawn, eating large quantities of sweets and biscuits in the quiet evening period before he returned from work.

Ella made strenuous efforts to lose weight. Always being 'on a diet' became a feature of her life. Through the years, she attended Weightwatchers, or tried out new diets she found in magazines and books. She always lost weight - and always put it on again, and more. The only rest from this wearying struggle was during her two pregnancies, when she 'let go' and ate what she liked with little anxiety.

Her husband didn't take to family life, started drinking heavily, and finally left, with another woman, when the children were young teenagers.

Ella's father died in the same year as her divorce came through, and to her surprise and dismay she was devastated. But there was not time to grieve. Her mother, now suffering badly with rheumatism, became very dependant on Ella for transport, decision-making and moral support. Ella's life became a round of part-time work, caring for her two girls and the house, and supporting her mother. Her compulsive eating got worse, and although she kept smiling as usual, she began to feel that life wasn't worth living.

At last, she went back to her doctor. He had always seemed sympathetic, and she thought he might understand. But when she got into the surgery, she somehow found herself minimalising the problem. 'Everything's fine really - I just need to lose a bit of weight, that's all - no self-discipline, that's my problem!' The doctor gave her a diet sheet, and offered to weigh her regularly. She went home and wept, consuming a whole fruit cake and half a pound of cheese in the process. Later, a friend mentioned that counselling might be helpful, and Ella wondered——

People may eat compulsively at any age, and may well begin, like anorexics and bulimics, in adolescence. The compulsive eater has deprivation, subtle or overt, in her background. There is a spread across the age-bands here; it is not at all unusual to meet compulsive eaters who began to show their distress through eating behaviour at later ages, and continue it well into middle age or even beyond.

The compulsive eater eats more than her body needs. She probably eats a great deal of carbohydrate-rich food. Perhaps she describes herself, laughingly, as a chocoholic - or a pig. She is ashamed of needing to eat. So, while she will join in with family meals, often consuming a carefully measured portion of low-calorie food to show herself and others that she is really on a disciplined diet, in secret she helplessly stuffs biscuits, icecream, scraps off others' plates, meusli, golden syrup sandwiches, etc. In an emergency she may eat bizarre foods such as dry icing sugar, still-frozen food from the freezer, or even canned pet food.

She becomes adept at buying and eating quantities of food in secret. If she cannot easily get anything to eat she may feel driven to retrieving food from the rubbish bin, stealing, or using money which should be used for something else to buy food. She is very ashamed of this, because at bottom she is honest and conscientious. She may be in financial trouble; either just poor, or perhaps guilty about stealing or misusing other people's money.

She is someone who eats to hide her unhappiness. Sometimes the connection between feelings and eating is fairly clear; she says she eats when she gets upset. But many compulsive eaters are not aware of any link at all between their eating behaviour and their feelings about their life experience. Most compulsive eaters feel terrible about their lack of self-discipline. In response to your comment that their eating may be something to do with not being very happy in their lives, they say they have everything they could possibly want, and have 'no excuse' to be miserable.

The compulsive eater feels that she is a greedy undisciplined slob, out of control, a failure, and a liar. It follows that she is likely to have some of the symptoms of depression, and may be very depressed. Most people in compulsive eating distress are fixated on the wish to 'get slim'. This, they feel, will magically sort everything out. They may offer this to you as their aim in counselling - indeed as their only goal in life. They may not be very aware of feelings about other topics.

The compulsive eater feels, indeed, that she has no right to be unhappy, or to need anything at all. She smiles a lot, to prove that she is contented. One of the problems is that, unlike the anorexic or the bulimic, she can take in and keep food, but has a lot of difficulties with the boundaries around eating.

This applies even in practical terms. What does it mean to be hungry? She has probably forgotten long ago. What does it feel like to be full? She has ignored the signals for so long that she couldn't possibly say. She is only aware of the twin signals of an almost continuous need of food and an equally continuous fear and distrust of it and its effects.

The client is likely to have tried a lot of different diets and diet organisations, without losing weight. If she has, she has probably put it all back on - and more. Educated guesses indicate that 90-95% of people who lose weight in dieting gain it back. So she will be coming into counselling with a strong sense of failure.

Sadly, this sense of failure may have been exacerbated by doctors, who may have told her that she is damaging her health/they can't (won't) operate on her/she really should lose weight before she gets pregnant/no wonder she has a bad back. It follows that she may well have got into the habit of neglecting her physical health, not seeking help for any physical problem in case the business of weight is brought up again.

What doctors have told her about her weight may all be true, but nevertheless it adds to her sense of inadequacy and her expectation that health professionals will criticise her. It means that she will have to work just a little harder to trust you as her counsellor.

She will have trouble in relying on you. Trust is not something that comes easily to her. Typically, she is someone on whom other people lean. She is a wonderful carer. One notices a much higher incidence of compulsive eaters in the caring professions than in any other work. Compulsive eaters are also good at caring for children, elderly parents, or indeed anyone in their social circle who seems to need it. Their sense of their own needs is so ephemeral, and their sense of guilt so strong, that they put everyone else first. They spend their lives atoning for their fat and (they assume) ugly bodies and disgusting, uncontrollable appetites.

Anorexia nervosa

Case Study - Alison

Alison lives with her parents in one of those big houses at the posh end of town. There's an old pony in the paddock, and a housekeeper in the kitchen. But Alison can't appreciate the luxury of her life. She's 28 now, but you'd never know it - she looks sixteen. She went to a London art school, and did very well. Now she works in a local graphic studio. Her work is good - when she's there. But increasingly, she's having days off.

Alison's been losing weight, quietly and insistently, for the past six years. Now she's down to about six and a half stone - pretty thin for a woman of 5'6". Her periods have stopped. She's cold all the time. Sometimes she wears a lot of loose, floppy layers, and fingerless gloves. But sometimes she slips on a glossy leotard, proud of her hard, lean body.

It's nobody's business if she's getting slim. She still feels a bit pudgy around the waist and thighs, but if she really works at it, one day she'll be really elegant. She's spending a lot of time at the gym, and goes to an aerobics class twice a week. She also has an aerobics tape at home, which she works out with every evening.

Alison has to have the same amount of food at each meal. Long ago she declined to eat with her parents, although sometimes, terrifyingly, her father will shout and rage at her to eat more. She must eat at exactly the same time too. She gets fearful and panicky if a meal is delayed for any reason.

It was when she was fifteen that Alison's younger brother, aged twelve, was killed in a car accident. Her mother was depressed for years - perhaps still is. Her father, a vigorous man who liked to stay in control, worked even harder at his high-level job, and said little. Her brother's name was seldom mentioned again. Noel was handsome, blond and funny, the darling of the family, and as her mother once said, 'suddenly the light was put out'. Now, Alison wonders if her parents' marriage was 'put out' too. Her mother spends a lot of time complaining about her father to Alison.

Alison can't bear to look into the future. She couldn't possibly leave her parents. Although men sometimes ask her out, she tries to avoid it. They might ask her to have a meal with them, and that, of course, would be impossible. She thinks that if only she can get down to a reasonable weight - just another few pounds - things might be all right. If only she can endure the terrible, gnawing hunger. Sometimes this seems to be eased by looking at all her cookery books, or even making a meal for her parents. But they don't seem to want her to cook for them any more.

What they do want, they've just said, is for her to go to the doctor's. She's been before, but he wanted to weigh her, and she wasn't having that! He might even want her to have tests, or go into hospital, and she's sure - well, almost sure - there's nothing whatsoever wrong with her. But in the quiet of her luxurious bedroom, she cries. There is something wrong, and she doesn't know what, or why, or how to put it right. Someone at work had the nerve to leave the Eating Disorders Association card on her desk. She might ring them when no one else is around——

*****

The anorexic (or, as some people say, anorectic) person is more likely to be a young person; anorexics have been reported as young as ten years old. The typical case is of someone of about sixteen or seventeen, but there are many anorexic people around much older than this, persistently maintaining their low weight amid much locked-in distress. From various studies, around three or four percent of women are thought to have full-blown anorexia or a partial form of it, especially amongst dancers, models and others whose jobs reflect the wish to conform to the female stereotype.

'Anorexia', meaning 'loss of appetite' is a misnomer. People with anorexia have not lost their appetite. They control it magnificently; such control is like an art form. Indeed Sheila MacLeod called her perceptive book on the subject, The Art of Starvation.

In practical terms, someone with anorexia keeps herself at a low weight, constantly striving to reduce it even further. She normally does this by controlling her food intake alone, rather than using vomiting or purging as a means of weight control. She erects around herself a scaffolding of expertise on food and its dangers. She may eat a regular, though small, amount of any food as long as she knows how fattening it is and it squares with her careful day-by-day calorie accounts. Or she may find it safer to eat the same food, in type and amount, according to the day of the week, or even the same food, in type and amount, every day. Some anorexics feel that it's only safe to eat exactly the same thing at exactly the same time every day, and some may carry this ritualisation even further by having to eat in the same situation, perhaps alone in the kitchen or the car, from a certain plate, or in front of a certain TV programme.

It is also very common for the anorexic person to become addicted to exercise - not the healthy and relaxing walk or swim that many of us enjoy, but a hectic, planned pattern of running, working out in the local gym, or following a video tape of exercise alone in her room. This is not done for enjoyment but in order to keep her weight down or lose more. Sometimes she says it is to 'get fit', but this is anorexic-speak for 'get thinner'. The exercise has a driven, fearful quality about it. Eating and exercise can fill the horizon completely for the anorexic person. 'If I eat X, I'll have to swim 20 lengths, but on the other hand I've got to eat a meal in public tonight, so I'd better make that 50 lengths, just to make sure of things', is a calculation of the sort that goes on all the time in her mind. The exercising is encouraged by the hyperactivity and 'high' sense that come with a starvation diet.

Alongside this behaviour, she has to deal with her body as it is. She will probably see it as fat and horrible, her thighs huge and her bottom laughable. If only she could lose 'just a few pounds', she believes her life would be transformed. But often she is on the light side, at one end of the scale, or emaciated at the other. She has a distorted body image.

Carrying too little weight means that her body will be an uncomfortable vehicle for living in. If she sits on a hard chair she becomes sore. Her muscles waste, and after a while she loses her physical strength and will eventually have to cut down or stop exercising, even if she is addicted to it. She is cold most of the time; her thick, loose layers of clothes not only disguise how thin she is, but also serve a purpose in keeping her warm.

If the behaviour worsens, her skin may become rough and dry; her hair will get thinner and her nails become brittle. Her blood pressure will drop, her periods will stop and she will become sterile. There are various biochemical abnormalities. She will probably have sleeping problems; starvation keeps any animal alert for food. Osteoporosis is possible. Mortality is thought to be 10-19% - half from suicide, and half from starvation.

The anorexic person was, typically, a 'good' child, from what she will probably tell you is a 'perfect' family. Never did she rock the boat. Usually intelligent and hard-working, she lived up to all expectations, keeping any incongruence or unhappiness locked away inside herself.

It's interesting how often words to do with prisons, cages and locks come up in discussing anorexia. The anorexic really is caged in eating distress. Her behaviour is likely to cause uproar and desperation amongst her family and friends, who will probably see it as perverse and incomprehensible self-destruction. Because of concern for her welfare, pressure will be put on her to eat more. She will react to this in a range of ways.

She will almost certainly have to become secretive. Many anorexic people are mistresses of illusion, appearing to eat food which has really been secreted in a pocket or handkerchief. Or there will be 'reasons' why she needn't have a meal this evening, thank you - she has eaten at school, at a friend's house, at work. She is going out for a meal. She isn't hungry. She has a stomach upset. If the worst comes to the worst, this pacific, unassertive woman may be forced into rage and confrontation. She wishes everyone would leave her alone. Nobody seems to understand that the possibility of gaining weight terrifies her. Losing control of the appetite which rages within her is like a horrifying fantasy of obliteration.

Bulimia nervosa

Case Study - Lisa

Lisa is bulimic. The fact rules her life. She is 23, and works in a garage office, dealing with orders for spare parts. She lives in terror lest her workmates (especially the men) think she is fat, or eats too much. She avoids talking much to anyone at work.

At home, she lives with her parents, her younger sister, and an uncle who is partially disabled and has always lived with the household. He is her father's brother. Her mother dislikes and resents him, which causes constant rows and an unhappy atmosphere. Her mother is a powerful person and this matter is just about the only one in which she doesn't get her own way.

Lisa was teased at school for being fat and having frizzy red hair. Sometimes her sister teased her too. She learned to keep out of the way of her schoolmates, or, when she had to be with them, she developed a passive, 'anything-to-keep-the-peace' attitude which hid her underlying attitude very satisfactorily.

In her last year or so at school she lost weight dramatically, and her teachers began to notice that her work improved too. She was really good at maths and science, turning in immaculate homework which had clearly taken hours to complete. But when it was suggested that she might like to go on to the sixth form, she declined, refusing to talk about her reasons.

She was almost fifteen when she learned the trick of making herself sick. A year later, she plucked up the courage to buy some laxatives from Boots. Now she could stuff herself with all the food in the fridge - plus the chocolate, crisps and cakes which she brought home in carrier bags - and never put on weight. It was difficult, but her figure was all she had ever wanted.

Now she has a routine. She does without breakfast. She's starving hungry by lunchtime, and she goes out to buy herself several pork pies, and often a whole battenburg cake. She varies the shops so that the shop assistants don't become suspicious. Sometimes she gets some Mars bars too, if she's got enough money. [To her shame, she sometimes steals them if she hasn't]. She locks herself in the office loo, and stuffs all this down, being careful not to rustle paper in case anyone else is around. Then she drinks a lot of water. Within minutes, she can go back into the cubicle and vomit the lot down the toilet. Then she washes her hot face, and goes back to work.

In the evening, Lisa's expected to eat a 'proper meal', as her mother puts it. Meat and two veg, and a pudding. Lisa is a good girl and does what she's told. But as soon as she can escape, she drifts upstairs to her bedroom and swallows between thirty and fifty laxative pills. Later in the night the cramps grip her and, while the household sleeps, she can get rid of all that food in the toilet. She often looks very tired. She never goes out in the evenings.

Lisa's doctor knows about her. But somehow Lisa can never stick with any help. She's wondering, now, about trying counselling. But what good would that do, just talking? She's desperate. Perhaps killing herself would be better than revealing the disgusting world she carries inside her——

*****

Bulimia - 'eating like an ox' is neither a particularly helpful nor a very well-known name. It's common for people to get it wrong and be unsure of what it means. Workers don't help, because they use variations like 'bulmarexia' (which isn't wrong in itself; it's just that different names for a complex syndrome confuse everyone even more). For the purpose of this booklet I'll use 'bulimia nervosa' or 'bulimia'. It's estimated that about 2% of women of reproductive age are bulimic (100,000 in the UK), plus 4-5% with a partial syndrome.

The essential features of bulimia are bingeing, vomiting, often together with abuse of laxatives, or sometimes (more rarely) diuretics. And as I write here at my word-processor, I realise with amazement that I am replicating what people with bulimia do. I tried to describe in a word-picture a representative compulsive eater, a typical anorexic; yet when I come to the bulimic I start to distance myself from the real person, talking in more academic terms: 'the essential features of bulimia are—'

People with bulimia do this to themselves all the time, pushing the real, messy, emotional human side of them over there somewhere, keeping what they feel are the acceptable features to the front and leaving the rest in the bathroom. Let me start again.

Although people with bulimia may be of any age from fifteen or so onwards, the bulimic client is most likely to be a young working woman with high standards for herself. Her sense of duty to her family and her work is striking; she finds it very difficult to be assertive. She feels that, in order to live up to her high standards, her body must be lean and fit in line with the rest of her life.

The problem is that life isn't really like that. Within her are uncomfortable emotions, resentment, anger, sexuality, neediness. She is not neat, lean, self-contained and successful all the time. And those 'unacceptable' feelings terrify her. She tries even harder to squash them. She starves, but that makes her feel ill. Eventually she is driven by her unruly body to stuff herself with food. That's even more terrifying; now, unless she does something about it, she will be fat. She can get rid of the food;

she learns to make herself sick. And perhaps a bright idea strikes her; if she uses laxatives she will be able to expel the food that does manage to make its way into her gut.

So the woman eases her way into a cycle which then takes over like a machine. The binge, while it satisfies, temporarily, the craving for food, becomes tailored for vomiting later. Some bulimics make sure they begin with a coloured marker, tomato juice for instance, so that when they vomit later, they can see that everything has been ejected. Plenty of fluid helps the vomiting; a binge is often finished off with large quantities of coffee, diet Coke, or water. The client may eat and vomit several times a day, or at the other extreme she may only feel the need to vomit when she has eaten a particularly large meal for a celebration, or perhaps in the pre-menstrual period when she is feeling particularly vulnerable. The key characteristic is that, like the compulsive eater and the anorexic, she is constantly and exhaustingly on edge about her weight, appearance and food.

She is never able to have a rest from the cycle because each phase leads on to the next. If you starve, you are desperate to eat; when you binge, you must vomit it out, or you'll get fat; now you've got rid of it, you will be hungry again soon, and then you've got to face the fearful decisions about what and how much to eat. And in between, and round the edges, are the temptations to make getting thinner easier by using the laxatives, or fitting in yet another aerobics class, or running, or swimming. Your world becomes an endless, inescapable turning wheel in which you are trapped with fewer and fewer choices.

The bulimic may well be regularly using large quantities of laxatives. It is not uncommon to hear that the client is taking fifty, a hundred or even more a day, and suffering long painful times in the lavatory as a consequence. If the bulimia has taken this much of a hold, there are some serious physical effects which may happen. Menstrual disturbances are common. There is a possibility of dental erosion, and parotid gland enlargement which gives a rather moon-faced appearance to someone who has recently binged and vomited. Damage to the Ÿsophagus, sometimes giving a husky voice, and dilation of the stomach may also occur. Dehydration and the accompanying loss of minerals, potassium and so on may precipitate renal damage, fits, and cardiac arrythmias. At its worst the syndrome can be lethal.

The person with bulimia may well be somebody who is tempted to other kinds of fast-results behaviour too. Alcohol, drugs, compulsive spending or shoplifting, these kinds of things may be seductive and add their own painful complications. On the other hand, it is just as likely that the client will be upright, well respected, socially skilled and a high achiever in whichever field she occupies, keeping the bingeing/vomiting behaviour as a closely-guarded secret.

Common factors - the binge and other things

The binge exists for everyone in eating distress, either as a reality, as often for the compulsive eater or the bulimic; or as a horrifying fantasy for the anorexic. Bingeing means eating a lot of 'illegal' (calorie-rich) food. 'A lot' means different things for different people. For the very controlled bulimic, a binge may consist of a couple of peanut butter sandwiches and a banana. At the other end of the scale, a binge may be a supermarket trolley full of crisps, chocolate, cheese, gateaux, ice-cream, bread, butter, cream and sweets.

An important feature of a binge is its secrecy. No one else must even suspect the eater. For this reason enormous lengths are often gone to to ensure that the person has privacy. The binge begins when the person decides to binge. This may be some time before the buying, preparing and eating starts. Once the decision has been made the urge and determination to eat builds up steadily to an enormous psychological excitement and pressure. If interrupted, the person may turn on the unwitting culprit with ferocity.

Bingeing is often a messy, voracious business in which the eater stuffs food down as fast as possible. There are no rules about how or what she may eat. She may well not use plates or knives and forks; she may tip out the items chaotically and move from sweet to savoury, hot to cold, creamy to crispy, taking the food out of their papers or containers as she fancies like a small hungry child satisfying her longing. She may eat standing up, stuffing the food in with feverish urgency, perhaps near the rubbish bin in case anyone comes in. It is mixed bliss and terror.

After eating, if the person is bulimic, she will probably find a way of making herself sick and/or using laxatives. If she is a compulsive eater, she will just go to sleep, only to wake to a nightmare of dread and guilt at all those pounds she has put on.

It is essential to understand the conviction and urgency with which the person pursues their particular kind of eating behaviour. Many health professionals try and suggest that the person just stops doing it, or uses more will-power. This is worse than useless; it is actually destructive in that it reinforces the person's sense of helplessness and failure when, as is inevitably the case, she's unable to comply. Even if she is able to stop the behaviour temporarily by an effort of will, it will almost certainly recur unless the reasons for it have been understood and she has developed new ways of expressing herself.

There are some other general points which apply to all the forms of eating distress. Many people with these disorders are survivors of child sexual abuse, often incestuous. As well, alcoholism or other addictive behaviours often exist in the person's family of origin. Some years ago it was noticed that a large number of anorexics, in particular (although it might apply to people with bulimia and compulsive eating as well) had 'family secrets' in their backgrounds. By this it was meant that there were such things as divorce (when it was scandalous), suicide, abandonment, sudden death and so on, which were never explained or discussed within the family.

All of these phenomena give rise to a familiar pattern of behaviour in families. The key word is silence. In such families, people neither feel, nor think, nor speak about the distress. By some mysterious process, the 'happening' (whether it is incest, violence, scandal, grief, alcoholism or whatever) is silenced out of existence. It may be continuing to happen; but all the family members suppress any kind of acknowledgement of it, either inside or outside themselves. This pattern of behaviour is likely to continue even when the person is an adult, and if the client has indeed endured any of these things in her family of origin you will have particular, characteristic issues to deal with in your work together.

Some issues around diagnosis

It can be helpful to have an idea of whether the client you are working with is bulimic, or anorexic, or a compulsive eater. But it is worthwhile taking care not to jump to any conclusions! There are various reasons why mistakes can be made, and the consequences of these may be that counsellor and client misunderstand each other quite disastrously.

Firstly, the client herself may be so anxious about eating that she tells you that she is a compulsive eater. Bear in mind that anyone in eating distress is, per se, anxious about eating at all, let alone too much. Bear in mind also that you cannot tell by weight (except at the extremes) what is going on for the person. She may think of herself as a compulsive eater, while, for example, vomiting, using laxatives, or keeping herself on a starvation diet.

Secondly, there is some assurance if your client arrives with a diagnosis from a doctor. However, doctors cannot be specialists in everything, and the patient may not have told her doctor all the facts. It's best not to rely too heavily on a medical diagnosis.

Thirdly, there is a range of differential diagnoses around eating. For example, many people 'go off their food', or eat more, when dealing with a stressful life event. Most of us would agree that such reactions are part of the individual's internal economy and generally need not be viewed as problematic in themselves.

More seriously, there are other reasons why people experience changes in appetite, and some of these are due to physical illness. Obviously counselling alone is not appropriate if physical illness is the cause - and it could even be fatal if the illness is serious and the client relies on counselling rather than medical help. However, if this is the case it should become clear to you fairly soon, as you realise that the other main strands of eating disorders are absent - for example, the obsession with weight and getting thinner, and the characteristic desire for secrecy around eating behaviour.

From the counsellor's point of view, diagnosing any particular disorder is not, of course, vital, but it does give some basis for understanding what kind of experience the client is going through. However, people seldom fit into artificial categories and the important thing to do is to listen and try to understand, rather than to make labelling the client's problem your first concern.

In any case, there is huge variation in how individuals behave, and the categories of eating distress merge into each other in many ways. In practice people may binge and vomit for half the week and starve the other half; or eat compulsively for nine months of the year and live on a proprietary chemical mixture for the other three months; or starve all day and fill up with everything in the fridge at nightime; or 'yo-yo' between 'being good' (ie. following a strict diet) and either bingeing or using a variety of bizarre ways of eating. Laxatives, diuretics, and compulsive exercise may be entwined with all these behaviours. But again, many people do more or less conform to the generally accepted divisions of eating disorder.

Whatever the form your particular client's eating distress takes, your main task as a counsellor will be to help her to link her eating behaviour with her feelings about her life experience, and to express those feelings more appropriately.

Principles of Good Practice

It isn't easy to summarise in a neat list what should and should not be offered in working with people in eating distress. Every client is different and has different needs; in general, guidelines are more appropriate. But there is one overriding principle, from which all the others flow. That principle is that each client is approached with respect, compassion and acceptance. When working with a client in eating distress, that acceptance will include the acceptance of behaviour and appearance which the client herself finds hard to accept; namely, her eating behaviour and body size and shape, as well as of the inner self, the self beneath the eating distress.

Choice

In the preliminary stages of meeting and working with your client, there are several things to take into account. To begin with, the client should refer herself rather than be referred. This is because, right from the beginning, it is important to be sure that she does want to meet a counsellor, and secondly, that it is you she wants to see. Since control is such an important issue for people with eating problems, everything possible should be done to make sure that 'the system', relatives, or friends, don't begin insidiously to establish an authoritarian structure before your client even gets to meet you.

So she herself makes the initial appointment at a time which is convenient to you both. In the first session, she should be made aware that she still has choices. For example, she may prefer to see a man rather than a woman, a group rather than an individual, or to see you on another day. While it isn't always possible to give her just what she wants, a meeting should be encouraged in an attempt to do so.

This will give your client an early message of respect for her as an individual. For she will almost certainly be terrified of bringing you her most shameful fears and neediness, and will be glad of all the space she can get to pull her dignity around her.

Consistency and boundaries

Every effort should be made to offer consistency from the beginning of counselling. That is, if possible, the same counsellor should be available at regular intervals, preferably weekly, on the same day, at the same time, and in the same place - or adapting to the client's schedule if necessary, for instance if she is on shift work. This may seem obvious, but can be a problem, for example in a hospital or surgery counselling. Even more difficult, but vitally important, is the need to offer counselling for as long as necessary, so that your client does not feel hurried, starved or deprived of what she needs.

This is of particular help to the person in eating distress, who will have difficulties with boundaries around taking in good things. She will find it reassuring to know that your attention and care is dependably there when she expects it to be; that it begins at a certain time and (equally important) finishes at a certain time; and that you mean what you say and will not let her down without very good reason.

For the client, counselling will seem like food, with all the complexities of her relationship with it built into her relationship with you. To feel safe, she needs to know that you are there for her and that she is safely contained within firm boundaries.

While the issue of boundaries is vital for all clients, it is especially salient for people with bulimia, who find it distressing and confusing if you aren't clear about what you can and can't offer, what is and isn't negotiable. This will also apply to the question of payment, if this is involved in your practice. For people in eating distress the question 'who has the power?' is ever-present. For people with bulimia in particular, their own ambivalence about counselling trips them up often enough; being unsure where your limits are makes counselling very difficult indeed for both of you. It is helpful to be both clear and realistic about where your boundaries are.

Taking the eating behaviour seriously

People in eating distress are well used to being trivialised or dismissed. Your client's experience of counselling should be different. Her concern about her eating, food, weight and appearance should be taken absolutely seriously. Whatever she thinks is relevant, whatever she brings into the session, is relevant and valuable.

This means that, instead of making your own judgement of the person's appearance - for example, she looks of average weight, is rosy-cheeked and bright-eyed, therefore she can't be *really* ill - you listen to the underlying concerns. She may look fine, but she feels bad around food, and wretched about her appearance. That is the psychological reality, and that is what you, together, will take seriously.

As the sessions continue, it is important to give full value to the eating behaviour. It should not be treated as an arbitrary and perverse behaviour which should be stopped as soon as possible. In fact, there are often times when it might be more helpful to be accepting and encouraging about the behaviour, strange as this may seem to the client. Paradoxically, valuing the behaviour allows the client to breathe deeper, to relax and look about her, to think more seriously about this position she is in, and to trust you to look with her.

What you may both be able to recognise, after a lot of looking and exploring in this frantic wheel of eating distress, is the function of the behaviour itself. It is often very helpful for the client to realise that she isn't crazy or 'mentally ill'. This seemingly incomprehensible behaviour has a function; there is a perfectly understandable internal logic going on.

The behaviour may have one or more of several functions. At its most simple it expresses feelings which may be inexpressible in any other way. Often, it encapsulates in metaphor or a kind of poetry what is meant. It can act as proxy for the real issues, those issues of pain, or despair, loss or oppression which gave rise to the distress in the first place. It may be a way of denying these issues, distracting attention from them, or even attempting to replace them altogether, by indicating to the woman and those around her 'the problem isn't that I'm a survivor of child sexual abuse (or whatever) - no, I'm an anorexic, that's my problem'.

Whatever the function of the distress for this particular person, one of the tasks of counselling is to clarify it, talk about it, and understand it together.

Liaison with doctors

If you aren't medically qualified, you and your client together will need to discuss the issue of liaison with a doctor. It may be that your client is already seeing her GP regularly, and s/he may be quite happy for their patient to be seeing a counsellor. Or it could be that your client is physically fit and not really putting herself in physical jeopardy. In this case it is of course up to her to visit her GP as and whenever she wishes.

However, it's often the case that you're working with someone who, you feel, may be threatening her health by her behaviour. For example, someone with a very low or very high body weight; or someone with severe bulimia, who may become badly dehydrated in the course of vomiting or purging. Your own confidence and experience in working with people in eating distress will also be a factor.

If you're worried or concerned at all, then it is wise to discuss with your client the possibility of linking up with a GP who will monitor her health while you are working with her. Ideally, it's good to maintain a three-cornered partnership between you, your client and a sensible GP who is aware of the long time-scale of most of this work and isn't going to be alarmed if your anorexic client isn't plump and rosy in six months - even better, one who knows that the weight of the patient isn't the salient point; her psychological health is.

The blessings of a really good GP are legion, and will make your own work very much easier. S/he can keep an eye on weight and general physical health, monitor blood if necessary, reassure anxious relatives, and generally act as a stable link between everybody concerned. In addition, s/he can also provide the safety net of hospital if that becomes necessary.

If your client agrees to this, you will need to talk with her about who she will go to. Naturally, her own regular GP is best provided she trusts him/her; and there are, regrettably, some risks about being open with some members of the medical profession about an eating problem, as I've mentioned in the Introduction. If your client is worried it's worth talking through who else she could see. Many surgeries have several doctors, and patients are welcome to see anyone they choose, or it may even be a good idea to change surgeries. Your client may have difficulty with this, as, with the typical diffidence of the person in eating distress, she may worry about 'offending' her regular doctor if she sees somebody else.

Take your time though. It's important to get this sorted out before you get properly started. You may even wish to consider how firm you want to be regarding the need to see a doctor regularly. As a non-medical counsellor, if I'm feeling at all worried about a client's physical health, I present the need to liaise with a doctor as my usual practice, and refuse to take the person on for counselling unless she is willing to take a GP into her confidence and see him/her as often as seems appropriate. I'm willing to go to a good deal of trouble to help the client find a doctor she can feel safe with, but that's the bottom line.

Confidentiality

This may seem too obvious to be stated; lesson one in every counselling training course. But you will be surprised at how pressing and reasonable the requests of others for a 'progress report' can seem. Relatives and friends, and even other workers, can become unbearably anxious about the client, and sometimes find it very difficult to understand the principle of confidentiality in counselling. Parents ring up wanting to know how they should react to their child's behaviour, how best to help her, and how she is getting on. Workers contact you to let you know what your client has done, or said, so as to 'help you to work with her better'. Anorexics and bulimics particularly have a most extraordinary effect on their social circles; everyone wants to help, comment, and do **something**, anything - and that often means contacting you, the counsellor.

Nevertheless, just as with any other client, you have to keep the relationship between you clean. You are gently but firmly discouraging to everyone else, because you are there for your client, to help her 'explore, discover and clarify ways of living more resourcefully and towards greater well-being'. You do not disclose anything whatsoever about your client to anyone else - not even whether she is coming to sessions or not. You show her any letters about her which go between you and her GP (see above). She is your primary concern.

There are some very specific circumstances in which you may wish to break this rule. These are, if she is threatening suicide or hurting others, for example children. It may then be necessary to consult with her GP or others - but only after letting her know that you are going to do it, and why.

Notes on work with people with specific eating syndromes

Compulsive eaters are frequently under quite reasonable pressure from medical workers to lose weight. This may be to alleviate problems like varicose veins, backache, or high blood pressure. Or it may be to make surgery easier, prepare for pregnancy, or improve or avoid illnesses like diabetes or gall bladder problems.

If the woman who is a compulsive eater comes into counselling with 'losing weight for medical reasons' on the top of her agenda, counsellor and client together need to explore what the client expects from counselling. Compulsive eating is just what it says, and if the counsellor goes along with the 'will-power theory' (that you can make yourself diet without taking note of psychological processes) this will ricochet the client back into isolation, stuffing and failure. Dieting is fine for people who do not have these psychological eating problems. It is certainly not to be encouraged if the client is a compulsive eater, or bulimic or anorexic for that matter.

It must be clearly recognised that the client is unable, at present, to stop herself from overeating, which is why she has come to counselling in the first place. The psychological reasons for the behaviour are so pressing, and her need to be heard so great, that listening to the underlying distress has to take top priority. It must be dealt with first.

This will mean that weight loss will probably (though not necessarily) come later, once the client is able to nourish herself appropriately. Her anxieties about losing weight should be heard and given full value, but should not panic the counsellor into suggesting diets or urging the client to stop overeating.

Anorexia nervosa requires patience in both counsellor and client (not to mention relatives, friends, and medical workers). When the client is in the throes of the distress, she will only admit you into her inner world if she is sure you are safe. She has to be quite convinced that you are not about to trick her into getting 'fat' by arguing with her, bullying her, or reporting her to the hospital or whatever - and that none of these is your long-term aim either.

Working with an anorexic client is like sitting with someone who is inside a cage, cramped and miserable. The key to the cage is lying within her reach, just outside on the ground. You, too, are just outside the cage, sitting peacefully, keeping her company. Your aim is not to force the key into her hand, for she can pick it up herself if she wishes. You are there to explore with her the cage itself, why she got into it, and what she fears if she came out, and to maintain your faith in her decision-making ability.

There are more detailed issues about people with anorexia who are maintaining low body weight, which will be discussed in the following section.

Bulimia nervosa sufferers need clarity and gentleness from you. The clarity is important because, as mentioned above, bulimia muddies boundaries and perception. As a counsellor, you need to be very clear about your own identity, remain well grounded in sessions, and be aware that the client needs to feel safely contained.

The gentleness and acceptance is important too. The client is managing to live her life with a symbolic brick wall dividing her in half. On one side of the wall is her 'good' and acceptable side. One the other are all the dirty, nasty, frightening and 'bad' feelings. The task of the counsellor is to help the client to integrate all these sides of herself into the rounded human being she really is. To do this effectively, you yourself have to see her as whole and her behaviour - all of her behaviour - as completely acceptable.

This is not easy when the client herself, in all her words and feelings, is rejecting the bulimic behaviour as well as the life-circumstances and feelings she is afraid of. It will require slow, patient and empathetic work, which necessarily has to take account of the deepest feelings of fear the client brings to the sessions.

Using resources

If you aren't used to working with people in eating distress, it is sensible to use any further resources you may need to help you deal with the pressures and questions of this kind of work. Your first resource will be your supervisor. For further information and ideas, there are many books on this topic, and some of these are mentioned in the bibliography.

The following two organisations are also most helpful:

The Eating Disorders Association & National Information Centre, Sackville Place, 44 Magdalen Street, Norwich NR3 1JE.
Tel: 0603-621414
Offers a telephone helpline and information to do with anorexia nervosa and bulimia nervosa. Also a regular newsletter for people with eating disorders, and a journal for workers, the *British Review of Bulimia & Anorexia Nervosa*. This organisation will also talk to relatives, etc. and is therefore an invaluable referral resource. EDA also helps to set up and support self-help groups across the country.

The Women's Therapy Centre,
6 Manor Gardens, London N7 6LA.   Tel: 071-263 6200.
Special expertise in all the eating disorders. Programme of workshops including topics around eating distress/body image etc., well worth attending for both counsellors and their client. Short-term training for professionals.

Issues for the Counsellor

The counsellor's priority is to help the client to link the unhappiness in her life with her eating distress, and to find new and more life-enhancing ways of expressing how she feels.

One of the most seductive traps for a counsellor is to start telling the client what to do. Of course we know that we shouldn't do that. But in working with people in eating distress the pressures are immense. You can see (and the client often tells you, quite forcefully) that if only she could stop doing X then her life would be fine. If only she could eat a little more, just quarter of a slice of toast in the morning, that would be a start. Or, if only she could resist that terrible urge to vomit after just one of her meals, just once a week. Or, what else could she do instead of coming home from work and bingeing? Go swimming, perhaps? You want to encourage her, for her own sake, because you can see how unhappy her eating patterns are making her. She wants you to encourage her. She may ask you directly what she should eat or how she should behave.

But telling her what to do, or even encouraging her in a particular direction, isn't helpful. For one thing, if you slide away into completely concentrating on the food/weight issues, this will stop either of you from looking at what's underneath, at the things that really distress her. She may not have the words for these. She has put all her unhappiness, her sense of being out of control, her anxiety about her world, into a big pile and stuck a label on the top. The label says, in big clear letters: EATING PROBLEM. The label is the best she can do, and she believes it's true, but it's a mistake for the counsellor to swallow it whole!

For another thing, eating distress always carries a silent message about control. Chances are that the client has had a rough ride as far as control of her own life is concerned. She may feel that she is never in control. She may well be used to other people telling her what to do all the time. She probably reacts to the needs and expectations of others without even thinking about it.

Or maybe she's very angry about her unassertiveness - but still finds it impossible to change. If you as her counsellor fall into the trap of doing just the same as everyone else, presenting her with requirements and expectations, she will never be able to see what her pattern is and you will be denying her the chance to learn to make her own decisions.

However, your refusal to give your client direction may make her angry. Like many clients, she has probably come into counselling with great expectations (bolstered by family and friends) that now she will get some answers, now she will be told what to do to get better. It can be alarming to her to find that the work is rather different. Her anger is quite reasonable and healthy, and you can recognise this and work with it.

Valuing eating behaviour

All of this doesn't mean that you should treat your client's body size and anxiety about food with indifference. You can care about her bodily comfort and survival, and be interested in her eating and weight, and make that explicit, without making demands on her.

The behaviour in itself is very useful to you both in counselling because it gives you and your client clues about how to understand what is going on. It may be a living metaphor: 'I'm like a big solid heavy pyramid because my Mum and Dad fought over who should own me for most of my childhood, and I refuse to be split in half.' Or: 'I'm trying to satisfy all the conflicting demands on me. I'll eat, then get rid of it. I'll be fat and rebel, and thin and conform, all at once.' Or: 'I'm the very best at slimming. I'm so good that I deserve the very best care you can give me.'

The behaviour holds within it all the feelings the person is struggling to deal with. It needs to be taken seriously in its own right. Ultimately and paradoxically, it can be valued by the client as a life- and sanity-saving measure. It has very real meaning. It's helpful to the client (when she trusts you enough) to spell out in detail exactly how she binges/vomits/ uses laxatives and so on, and how she feels stage by stage.

Four strands of work

There are four strands to the work you and your client will do together:
- your client's life story and her feelings about it
- her relationship with food, her body, and the business of feeding herself
- her future
- and, if you are working psychodynamically, your relationship with each other.

These are like four strands of a plait, all linked together and interdependant.

To take these one at a time:

a) **Your client's life story and her feelings about it**
Of course you are interested in this, and your client will tell you about it naturally. But she will be careful. With people with eating problems, there is often an exaggerated loyalty to their family. Your client will skip over or make excuses for what may seem like appalling mistreatment, or tell you that she 'didn't really mind' when things happened to her which anyone else would be enraged or terrified about.

One of the familiar things you hear people with eating distress say is, 'Well, I suppose things were a bit difficult sometimes, but no worse than anybody else's life. I can't see why you're interested -' (in her uncle's sexual abuse of her/her mother's mental illness/her abandonment to distant grandparents at the age of ten, etc., etc.). It follows that it will take long, patient and very accepting work on your part to create enough safety for her to separate out the painful feelings from under the denial - and from the eating behaviour. Bringing out a feeling into the light of day will be enormously risky for her, and she needs to know that you are aware of this. It's likely that she will immediately be swamped with guilt if she says anything even remotely critical about her parents, for example, and this should be acknowledged, while recognising that perhaps these feelings are tolerable, and can be talked about.

Together, you can now begin to see some of the function of the eating distress. It's like a big sack into which your client can put all her sad, angry and painful feelings. When she closes up the neck and writes the label on it (the one that says 'Eating Problem'), she can't see the 'bad' feelings any more. It is helpful to talk about this in counselling in whichever way is most comprehensible to your client and comfortable to you. You can gently acknowledge that there are feelings 'inside the sack' between you, while assuring her that you won't press her or force her to reveal more than she is ready to deal with; she herself is in charge of what she talks about, and when.

b) **Her relationship with food, her body, and the business of feeding herself**
It isn't usually very difficult to get someone in eating distress to talk about this in general, rather vague terms: 'I binge terrifically at the weekends', or 'I feel huge - specially my thighs', or 'Mum's always

pushing me to eat more, and I don't like more than a salad at night'. However, one may need to ask rather more specific questions, very sensitively, partly in order to clarify just what is going on, but mainly in order to show your client that you are able to understand and accept the details of what she probably feels is intolerable, shameful behaviour. Having at least one other person (you) in on the secret is enormously relieving, especially if you show no signs of attempting to censor or stop her behaving as she does. You simply know and understand.

At some point, when it feels right, you will therefore be asking quite detailed questions about how much she feels she can manage to eat, or exactly how she makes herself sick, and so on. If you let your main concern be your empathy with the client's distress, you are unlikely to be put off by some of the extremes of behaviour which you'll hear; the huge quantities eaten by some compulsive eaters, for example, or the circumstances in which some bulimics are forced to vomit. You may be told about situations in which the client is denied private access to the toilet, for instance, and is forced to be sick into plastic carrier bags kept under her bed.

As far as the issue of body image is concerned, most people in eating distress are acutely aware of their bodies and have a distorted body image. Most feel that their body is too fat and not healthy (this means 'not slim enough'). For someone to whom bodies are the ordinary, variable, useful, skilled and, on the whole, pleasant enough miracles we live in, it may take a little time to tune in to the single note of the person in eating distress. To her, her body is ugly, fat and useless. No matter that it can write, read, swim, type, tie shoelaces; it may never let her down by being ill; she may have expressive eyes, lovely hair, beautiful hands. Nevertheless, because she feels she is fat, all this is irrelevant. A pound on makes her hate herself; being thinner, thinner, and thinner is all that matters. It can be heartrending, and sometimes confusing, to see your client looking bony and grey, telling you, with great conviction, how fat and disgusting she is.

Not only that, but apparently impossible moral burdens are loaded onto the gaining and losing of weight. Put simply, if you gain weight you are bad; if you lose it, you are good. This is true for any client in eating distress, from the most emaciated anorexic to the very overweight compulsive eater. What's more, the eldorado of 'being slim' or at target weight, is fraught with impossible fantasies. Yet asking your client how life will be when she's exactly as slim as she wishes to be produces oddly vague replies. 'I'll be much more confident' is the classic remark.

It is well worth exploring more precisely what she envisages when she's 'slim' (whatever that means to her), because maybe that vision doesn't really entail weight loss - perhaps she can make some parts of her ideal life happen no matter what weight she is.

It's also worth doing some work on why being the size she is now is good for her. Everyone is exactly the right size and shape for them at that particular moment in their lives. We all gain and lose weight as we need to; we build up a little fat in the winter, lose it in the summer. We may be fatter (or more gaunt) when times are tough, only to adjust, unconsciously, when we feel more comfortable in our lives. An awareness of this perfectly acceptable movement in the size we are can be most helpful to the person in eating distress, even though she will flip back very quickly into the neurotic 'thin = good, fat = bad' scenario.

So being the weight your client is at this moment has a meaning and a value for her. Probably, all she wants to do is reject her body. But it is worth presenting to her the idea that this body, now, at this very minute, is right for her. How is it helpful to her to be this weight? She may believe it happened by accident, 'because I'm greedy, or stubborn, or bad' or whatever. Yet, perhaps it's not those things at all. Perhaps it's because the weight has a purpose, carries a message for those around her, protects her from something, means something to herself or other people. Perhaps she feels angry or destructive towards those around her and this may include you, as her counsellor. This work is difficult and you may need to present it in different ways and at many different points in therapy.

Working on appetite can be especially helpful for the compulsive eater. It may be threatening for the bulimic or anorexic, however, since 'appetite' stands for both the lurking, shark-like danger of the binge and, at a deeper and even more dangerous level, the appetite for life which must recognise, as a prerequisite, the existence of needs. So we have to be careful and gentle when looking at these tender areas.

Hunger and its opposite, satisfaction, are worth looking at in the right circumstances though. What do you like to eat? (As opposed to what are 'good' and 'bad' foods). You could make lists of what is liked, what disliked. Many a client is surprised to find out what her tastes are! What does it feel like to be hungry? Full? What is your naturally preferred pattern of eating? Some of us like nothing to eat until 11 a.m.; others, lots of breakfast, then nothing till teatime. The point is, it depends on who we are and how we feel, not what the rules say.

This can, and does, feel quite frightening to the person in eating distress, who feels adrift in her needs and will cling on to any diet sheet, useless as it is, like a lifebelt. Yet we must learn, as the educationalist John Holt once wrote, to 'swim in uncertainty as a fish swims in water'. The counsellor can help her client to identify her needs, wants and appetites for food, as for other things, by calmly attending to and validating her feelings moment by moment throughout her sessions.

c) **Her future**

Another strand of the work you will do together is to do with looking at your client's future. How much control does she feel she has over what she does and what happens to her? Can she ask for what she wants? What is her 'ideal life' and how close can she get to it? Is it merely a fantasy or could she make it - or some of it - real?

It's quite surprising how many people have very little idea about planning and nourishing a good life. Many people in eating distress are so enmired in the struggle to survive that they have either given up hope of any kind of control or else their aspirations are unrealistic. The wish to be perfect is very common, and anything less is seen as a total, shameful washout. Interestingly, this reflects the attitude towards food: "I'm on a strict diet, and one tiny slip means I've failed completely; I might as well have an enormous binge". So part of your work together will be about formulating a realistic measure of what the client wants and how she can work towards it, both in the short and the long term.

d) **The relationship between you.**

How much you use this in your work will depend on your orientation as a counsellor. Your client will undoubtedly transfer feelings onto you from other relationships - she may work out her feelings about authority on you, feel deprived by you as perhaps she feels her mother deprived her, feel competitive with you as she was with her sister, and so on. Whether you enable her to use this or not is up to you and the way you work.

It can be very helpful to your client for you to be open about your feelings and thoughts in the sessions, provided they are for her benefit. Any distress of your own does not, of course, belong in your client's sessions. What she does need is the sense that you are able to understand and hold her distress, and will stay with her for as long as it takes, tuned in to her inner world.

Physical matters

Working with clients with these particular problems demands some knowledge and awareness of specific physical issues.

Starting with the simplest matters, people in eating distress are often sensitive to temperature. It helps your client if she is physically as comfortable as possible, so that in addition to your usual welcome, it's worth remembering that fat people are more likely to be too hot, while thin people may be chilly. The temperature in the counselling room could be adjusted accordingly. Similarly, people at the extremes of weight may find difficulty, say, in climbing stairs, and may need a discreet hand, or time to recover their breath if they have walked any distance.

Equally, some thought should be given to the chair you offer your client. Very fat people may be used to the embarrassment of not being able to fit into a chair with arms, or getting stuck in one, but they should not have to bear this humiliation in counselling. At the other end of the scale, very thin people will find it hard to sit on a less than comfortably padded chair for a whole session. It may seem trivial, but to a person at the extremes of weight it feels important!

Linked to this issue is the one of personal space. Many people in eating distress have some sexual abuse in their life story. For this reason alone, even a friendly hand on the arm on parting may be too much for someone for whom touch is frighteningly sexual. On the other hand, someone who feels bad about their body will probably be very aware of the wish for it to be accepted and comforted, and this may be an issue in counselling. These things may come up particularly if counsellor and client are of opposite sexes.

Medical Concerns

Counselling people with eating distress means also being alert to physiological problems. This doesn't mean weighing the client or taking over her responsibility for her own body. However, it's important to understand how the person's weight affects her mind and feelings and ability to work in counselling. It's also responsible counselling to try to stay aware of when the client may be in need of medical help, and we have looked briefly at the management of this in the section on 'Principles of good practice'. It isn't always easy to recognise when you should start to talk with your client about getting help from her doctor; frequently, especially with anorexics, you and the client are walking a tightrope together.

The bulimic client may not give such obvious physical signs of deterioration, but it is possible to become dehydrated quite quickly if both vomiting and laxatives are used, and if the bulimia is severe cardiac arrest is possible. Another complication, linked to this, is electrolyte imbalance, particularly the loss of potassium. Both bananas and orange juice contain potassium, and your client may be willing to take some orange juice, at least (bananas have more calories).

In someone with anorexia, the lower the weight falls, the more 'black and white' her thinking becomes. This can make counselling especially difficult. Someone locked into the need to keep losing weight, when she is already at a very low weight, requires a straightforward, yet sensitive approach and an awareness (shared with the client) that there may come a point at which she is no longer able to work in counselling. This is a point you will probably recognise if you are unfortunate enough to meet it. Your client will be withdrawn and unresponsive, unable to let you in at all. All her resources are directed towards keeping her alive; there is little or no free attention left for consideration of her situation.

This is the moment when you need to discuss with your client the possibility of asking her doctor for medical help. She should be seeing him/her regularly in any case. It may be necessary for you to contact the doctor (showing the client the letter) to say that you feel the client now needs medical help (which usually turns out to be hospitalisation), and that you will hope to continue counselling once the client's weight has improved enough for her to be able to work with you once more.

The prospect of hospitalisation is an issue which should be talked through in the last session or so, so that you can give your client as much support and choice as is reasonably possible given the circumstances. On no account should this be seen as a failure. There are all sorts of issues, both conscious and unconscious, feeding into your client's need to cling on to weight loss as the central meaning of her world. Neither of you are at fault.

There's a moment when you realise with a sort of cold shock just how serious this work can be; that girl who just left your counselling room could die. Because of the physical component, working with people in eating distress can sometimes be frightening beyond belief. This is completely understandable, and indeed a mark of your empathy with your client. It isn't a sign that you are too feeble to cope with this sort of work! However, what you do need to do, in order to stay balanced and maintain your faith in your client, is to find appropriate support for yourself at these times. A wise supervisor is, of course, particularly valuable when facing life and death issues of this kind.

You need to think through the issues around responsibility quite carefully when working with people in such difficulties - perhaps talking things through with your supervisor so that you are both as clear as possible about what kind of burden you bear.

Some of the questions you might consider are:
- What if your client is losing weight steadily?
- What if she collapses and is hospitalised or even, heaven forbid, dies unexpectedly?
- What if a suicide attempt is made?
- Should you insist on medical collaboration, even if your client is afraid of doctors or has lost all trust in them?
- Is there a point when you have to tell a client that you cannot work with them unless they put on a little weight - or at least stop losing it?
- What if your compulsively eating client is arrested for shoplifting?
- Or her diabetes worsens as she puts on weight, in spite of coming to counselling?

Having said all this, I have to add that, fortunately, it's rare to have to deal with such complex and stressful circumstances. Almost all clients seem to value counselling and are able to maintain a more or less steady weight until they decide to alter it, especially if they are able to consider the alternatives realistically.

The language you use

As your experience of working with people in eating distress increases, you learn that there are some things you simply don't say to your client. One of these is 'You're looking well', and similar phrases. It's all too easy to forget or slip out of the awareness of the altered world-view of the client in eating distress, and the acute sensitivity she has to implications from others about her weight and appearance. 'You're looking well' sounds inoffensive, even complimentary, to most people, yet it can feel like a dagger to the heart of the anorexic, bulimic, or compulsive eater. It means 'You're looking fat'.

More subtly, one has to remain very closely attentive to the client's feeling about weight change throughout counselling. It should be remembered that the client is likely to have many different feelings about this. One of the most common is the sense of surrender or capitulation to what others seem to feel is right. While the rest of the world is cheering as the anorexic gains weight, she herself may feel confused, frightened, resistant, or a spectrum of other colours of feeling.

Likewise, the fat person who is losing weight is noticing a wide range of changes about her body day by day. Part of her may be pleased, but it isn't as simple as that. Change requires adaptation, which takes effort and energy, and however much the person wishes the change to take place, and knows that it is healthy, there is also a strong sense of loss for the person she once was, and apprehension for what she might become. It is therefore not helpful for her to hear 'I think you've lost weight, well done' and similar 'encouraging' expressions.

These issues require great sensitivity from you as her counsellor. She relies on you to stay alongside her, helping her to come to terms with her feelings about change. Working over time with someone who is working very directly with her body and feelings together, draws out a need in the counsellor to be aware of the evolving process. The movement of feelings as weight changes, adaptation to the altered ways in which others view her, and the minutiae of a body which produces different responses and a different view in the mirror day by day, all these add up to an enormous, ongoing psychic effort which must be recognised as it goes along.

So your way of talking with the client will be empathic, taking into account all these things. As you open the door to her, you will be unlikely to comment on her looks, because even such a simple remark as 'You're looking better today' may alienate her from you before you even start the session.

Problems

Working with people with bulimia is fascinating. However, something you have to be prepared for is the enormous ambivalence with which the client lives. This almost certainly will affect the counselling work. The variations of behaviour which this ambivalence produces is huge. Clients come late, or don't arrive at all. They send letters of apology which arrive just after the missed appointment. They forget the cheque on payday. They forget the time of the session and arrive another time - when you have another client! They are unable to commit themselves to continuing work and dither onwards, a session at a time. And so on.

This can be extremely testing, and even exasperating. But remember that all this infuriating behaviour is not fiendishly thought up especially to needle you. It arises out of the deep terror the client feels about receiving something good and getting better. However, in order to stay poised and steady - and therefore of most use to the client - in the face of what can appear to be extreme provocation, you need to look after yourself as well as your client.

This means two lines of approach. Firstly, you can and should work on the ambivalence in sessions, listening to and recognising the client's fears and helping her to accept them. They are real and understandable, and it is fine to talk about them. Indeed it's very helpful to the client to talk about them, not in a persecutory tone but because they are part of the mass of her 'behind the wall' terrors. You may also need to be very straightforward, explaining that counselling is a process, the most fundamental part of which is that the two of you need to be in the same room together when you say you will, and that it doesn't work very well, and is a waste of her time and money, if sessions are missed or avoided.

Secondly, for your own sake, because you need to keep your own feet on the ground and have a job or a business to run, you need to be clear about exactly what you can manage and where your boundaries are. How many missed appointments will you tolerate from a new client, before you gently have to say no, I'm sorry, but you obviously aren't ready for counselling yet - contact me again when you're ready to come regularly? If you're in private practice, how many sessions will you give on credit, and what do you do about people who abscond owing money? These and similar issues may seem small, but they are vitally important in that they assure both your client and yourself that you can keep yourself safe and comfortable.

It's almost the opposite situation when working with people who are compulsive eaters. My supervisor used the analogy of a treacle pudding about one of my clients, after several sessions of stupefying sweetness which very effectively clogged up my awareness of the real issues. She was a lifelong compulsive eater who had learned, through the desperately deprived circumstances of her early life, that 'being nice' was all that mattered. Nothing else would get her through. It had been a wonderful strategy for survival, but was almost ruinous to any counselling work until I was alerted to it.

Having a client who is 'being nice' can be a treat. Compulsive eaters are inclined to come on time, pay on time, leap up to go a minute before the end of the session, and send you a postcard from their holidays. It is fatally easy to lean back and think that everything's going well.

The darker side of all this 'niceness' is that it hides sadness, anger, grief, despair and all kinds of neediness - from the client as well as the counsellor. You may find yourself colluding in the belief that everything's fine really - just this little problem of eating a bit too much. Inside, the client is screaming to be seen in all her pain. But the habits of a lifetime can form an iron carapace of pleasantness and good manners, just like the heavy armour of fat, which may prevent the counsellor from coming anywhere near the real and needy person within.

Working with this client, then, means listening very carefully to the music of the session, and not necessarily the words. It means trying to tune in to distress, which you can be certain is there given the expression of it by means of the eating behaviour; and not being deflected by the pleasant matter-of-factness your client may be showing. Here as nowhere else is the fear that if once she starts to weep, there will never be an end. Once she begins to show you her fear, and anger, and unhappiness, she will never be able to put it away again until next time. It's just too frightening.

It can be useful, then, to help your client to ground herself while she ventures into this dangerous territory. You may make a support chart together; help her to find a 'safe place' in relaxation; offer reading about others who have trodden this path; or talk with her about the way people can control the expression of distress, allowing it to come out, and then teaching her the tricks of 'putting it away' and coming back into everyday reality again. All or any of these or other safety-making devices may help her to see that she does not have to maintain the carapace all the time in counselling, and that you respect her need for protection as well as her yearning to be truly known.

This 'safety-making' is particularly helpful if, as is statistically likely, your client has suffered from abuse, sexual or otherwise, as a child or young person. If this is the case her self-esteem will probably be low and the eating distress may be one of several ways in which she sabotages her own life and potential success. Distress rooted in sexual matters may, understandably, grow into behaviour which affects the body and body-image. Being 'slim' (whatever that means to the individual client) carries meanings about sexuality in our society. It is worth exploring these carefully, and it may be necessary to work with your client on incidents of violence or other abuse, helping her to express her feelings and resolve the issues in whatever ways are most appropriate for your style of work.

It is never at all surprising to see some other issues emerge in this sort of counselling. Stealing or shop-lifting are quite common. Your client may admit this with a devastating sense of shame, perhaps some time after coming into counselling. The stealing may be from shops, or perhaps from friends or acquaintances. Stealing food is, of course, the most common situation, and some clients talk about a desperate need, not always acted upon, to take cake or other foods from the kitchen or dining-table of friends or relatives without being noticed, commenting as they tell you this that they are sure the hostess would have been delighted to give the item of food away if only she had been asked.

To find oneself doing this kind of thing is often very frightening, even more so than the out-of-control eating behaviour. It is against the law, and virtually always against the moral beliefs of the client too. When she finds herself doing this she is afraid she is going mad. Yet as always, once she has talked about it, some of the heat is taken out of the situation. In unfortunate circumstances, it may be necessary to support her through police prosecution. However, it is more likely that she has not been caught, and can allow herself to work on the problem in peace.

Another range of problems that is not uncommon, hand-in-hand with the eating distress, is an addiction to alcohol or drugs. How you deal with this in sessions depends on the client's point of view and your own expertise in these areas. Many workers would see these addictions as very similar to the addiction to eating behaviours - tailor-made to shield and drown inner unhappiness, and to be worked with accordingly.

However, you are likely to come across clients who, for instance, take Ecstacy a couple of times a month at 'raves' and feel there's nothing wrong in this; or alcoholics attached to AA, who are following the 12-step programme and believe that alcoholism is a physical disease. My own feeling is that the important thing is to reach whatever the client feels is the healthiest and most nourishing way of life for herself. If you as the counsellor are unsure of how to deal with particular issues, it is best to use your supervisor, and get expert advice or refer the client to it. Many towns have Alcoholics Anonymous, Councils on Alcohol, and drugs teams which are willing to advise and/or take clients for specialist work.

Groups and/or individual work

A lot of people in eating distress say that they'd like to meet other people in the same boat, and many counsellors may have the opportunity to offer their clients some group work. This can be very helpful, but if you decide to do it, it needs very careful planning.

There are three major kinds of group: the closed therapy group, the facilitated therapy group or the open group. An example of the closed self-help group is the kind which originated at the London Women's Therapy Centre (see address in the **Principles of good practice** section). This is a closed therapy group for either compulsive eaters or bulimics. Care should be taken not to mix the two, as the clash of different behaviours may set up discord in the group. Comprehensive booklets about running a compulsive eaters' self-help group and a bulimics' self-help group can be obtained from the WTC and are most useful for a small group of women wishing to form a group. Participants usually find these groups positive, supportive, and encouraging of insight.

People with active anorexia may find this kind of group very difficult, as they have very little free attention to give to other group members. It is usually best of offer individual work first.

Another style of group is the facilitated open group, of the kind run most successfully by the Eating Disorders Association. The central one is based in Norwich, but the EDA supports others across the country. The Norwich group is a large group, open to anyone with any eating disorder, their friends or relations, and anyone else with an interest in the topic. They meet fortnightly, often with an invited speaker. While the closed self-help group asks for commitment from its members, this group welcomes everyone, but people do not have to come regularly. There are at least two skilled facilitators.

If you have experience in running groups, you can offer a facilitated group using your own style, as many workers do. When you are planning it, it's worth reminding yourself that maintaining the clarity of boundaries is probably the most therapeutic activity you can offer. Therefore, be sure you have thought through (or negotiate with the group) such matters as timing, cost, minimum number of participants, finishing or review date, etc. and be very clear with every member of the group about what is expected of them in order to participate.

Experience seems to show that seeing individuals in therapy at the same time as working with them in a facilitated group, together with participants who are not the worker's clients, is not a good idea. If you have only a few clients with a particular eating problem, it seems to be best to direct them towards a group run by somebody else. There is no reason why such clients cannot remain in individual therapy at the same time as going to a group, as long as the underlying model of therapy is compatible.

A successful group is a joy, but groups can also be nightmarish - especially for the counsellor! It can be a hair-raising task simply to get enough people together for that first meeting. The ambivalence of group members can produce problematic situations in which you have to make difficult choices at a moment's notice. Participants may drift into 'politeness' rather than work. The facilitator has to hang on to the truth of the feelings in the meeting above all else, sometimes in spite of what is being said. It can sometimes feel like a thankless task.

On the other hand, a group can shift the client like nothing else. It can provide an environment in which the client can experiment with being bolder, braver and closer with other people than maybe she has ever been before. It can promote trust, courage and insight, and be an important therapeutic experience, the effects of which may last the rest of her life.

The counsellor's feelings

There are two strands of feeling in particular, which working with people in eating distress may provoke in you. One of these has to do with how you feel about your own body. Many counsellors working or wishing to work in this field have personal experience of eating distress. This can be very valuable in terms of the empathy with which you can work with the client, but it can also mean that you may internalise, unexpectedly, anxieties about the way you look and feel about your body, triggered by the client's own distress. You may notice this by the wish to go and eat, or even diet, after a session with someone.

Obviously it affects the client if she sees you changing shape over time, and though this cannot be avoided at times, for example if you become pregnant, or decide to lose or gain weight, her feelings about it may need to be discussed. What is important, however, is that you deal with your own distress outside the session, with your own supervisor or counsellor or whoever else is appropriate.

The other feelings often aroused in the counsellor are very basic ones, of the need to 'feed' thin and deprived clients with good things. You may catch yourself stuffing some unsuspecting anorexic with ever more rich insights or encouraging words, quite uselessly if they are untuned to her needs. More unpleasantly, there can be a punitive element in working with fat people, a sort of judgemental urge to stop them from 'indulging' themselves. This is a shock to notice in oneself, but essential to pick up and deal with. Fortunately clients seem quite able to be impervious to most of this, and you are unlikely to do as much damage as you may fear, provided you stay alert to your own feelings and deal with them appropriately.

Issues for the Client

Ideally, issues for clients and issues for counsellors are like two sides of a coin. But there are some concerns which your client may be carrying of which you may not, at first, be aware.

Power and control

For the client in eating distress, these are crucial issues. The whole syndrome of an eating disorder is an attempt by the person to empower herself. Controlling her bodily needs and weight is a symbolic attempt to control her life. So control is a central issue in eating distress, and it's crucial to pay attention to it in the therapeutic relationship.

The client is a consumer - both in the most obvious sense and of therapy. In the first instance we can assist her to take power in choosing a counsellor. It's a commonplace in counselling that we advise potential clients to select a counsellor carefully - but how possible do we really make this? Do we offer an initial 'taster' session without obligation, so that the client can sample our wares? Are we willing to encourage the potential, and almost certainly scared, client to ask questions about training, orientation, methods of work, years of experience, and so on, and do we answer openly, or do we mystify and 'psychiatrise' what we do? Do we have a knowledge of other workers in the area, and are we ready to offer this information? Are we willing, as individuals or institutions, to make public our orientation and methods so that clients have a real chance to choose someone they trust and with whom they can feel reasonably comfortable? These are actions and attitudes which will help to empower the person in eating distress.

Once the client is settled and committed to working with a particular counsellor, control continues to be an issue. Many new clients are weary and sick of their eating distress, sick of struggling with endless agonising decisions about what to eat and when, and deeply weary of failing, as they are bound to do, over and over again. They long to dump the whole thing in your lap, and for you to wave the magic wand and make them better. And as soon as they realise, appalled, that this won't happen - that working with you means just that - the fantasy of hospital comes up. How often has one heard the comment, 'I wonder if I ought to go into hospital - they could make me eat a proper diet, weigh me, stop me vomiting, just make me behave!'

The other side of this longing for someone else to take the reins is a deep terror of anybody else taking control. You as the counsellor may be seen as an all-powerful and dangerous god-like figure. Some clients take months to get over the dread of coming to the session each week for this reason. One can only be gentle and human, recognise these fears, and wait.

This wild swinging between different views of power echo the client's view of her own power. Chances are that she feels completely powerless most of the time. But there is also a deep sense of being too powerful - of being 'too big for her boots'. One day, she believes, something will catch up with her and give her her come-uppance. Guilt and terror fuel this feeling. But if all goes well, there will come a time when the client realises that you are simply an ordinary person there alongside her, trying to understand and to help. You are not an authority figure; neither are you a slavish employee. She can trust you to help while she retains complete control over herself. This is a vital stage in forging a truly therapeutic relationship.

Neediness

People in eating distress are fighting with the concept of neediness. Eating disorders in themselves are ways (ineffectual ones, to be sure) of trying to meet the person's emotional needs. So being in your counselling room - a concrete expression of need - makes your client feel extremely vulnerable; perhaps even more so than other clients. She is letting her neediness be seen.

For the person in eating distress, feeling needy - sad, hungry, lonely, sexual, wanting comfort, attention, or love - is a frightening thing, to be avoided at all costs. The problem with this viewpoint is twofold; one, that neediness is part of the human condition, and two, that if you won't let yourself recognise your needs you can never take action to have them met. Anyone who has ever sat with an entrenched anorexic, starving, hungry, cold and isolated, yet denying all these things, will have seen that this is true. Your heart goes out to her, yet she is unable to take anything from you. Her two greatest fears are that you will encourage her to get 'fat', or that you will somehow enable her to feel in need.

The roots of this attitude lie in needs unmet, by accident or design, in earlier life. If you have learned that whatever you hope for, want, or need, it may or may not come, regardless of what you do about it, you become hopeless and helpless. Being aware of needing just makes the pain worse, so you try your hardest not to be aware of what you want. The eating behaviour is a fine displacement, cover, or veil behind which to hide these impossible feelings.

In counselling, there will be a very unbalanced sense, of desperate unmet need on the one hand, and of a strong fear of dependency on the other. The client longs to be cared about, yet will the counsellor come too close and invade her space? As the client begins to get in touch with her own vulnerability, it's very frightening to think that the counsellor may not be able to cope with the immensity of her need. The client may think of herself as ravenously insatiable. If the counsellor finds out how bad she is, will she be rejected? All of these feelings are likely to be there in the course of counselling.

In the face of all this fear and confusion, it's a mark of the client's courage that she is sitting here in your counselling room, looking for help. Isolated and denying her own needs, the person has become a client in therapy - a last sign, perhaps, of hope. Perhaps you will be able to meet her needs. Better, perhaps you will be able to help her to articulate her needs and take hold of her power to care for herself.

Boundaries

The problem of establishing boundaries is exemplified in an eating problem. Literally, the person is confronting the issue of limits day after day. How much can she/should she eat? How fat or thin is she? Does she obey, or buck, the 'rules' - either those she has made for herself or those others lay down for her? There is no poise, steadiness or serenity in this day-by-day battle - no easy middle ground where she can take her size, shape and looks for granted.

So it's quite a problem for her to begin to develop a sense of herself. Who is she? What does she want? How does she separate herself and her needs and wishes from the needs and wishes of those close to her? Often she has developed advanced skills as a chameleon, and this can be quite noticeable in sessions. She's acutely aware of what you want, what you're driving at, what you'd like her to be, and she'll do her very best to adapt. It is very hard for her if your attitude is more open; if you are interested in what she wants, and is, and feels, she may be confused. She's afraid she'll annoy, or hurt, or simply be visible when she shouldn't be. It's hard for her to get a sense of herself as an individual, with rights and freedom of her own. 'Separation' gets confused with 'rejection'. So being different and separate, yet comfortable and accepted, is an unusual feeling for her, and something you can practise together in counselling. Out of this she may develop the ability to parent herself - to care for herself within her own boundaries.

The bulimic client

The bulimic client comes into counselling suspiciously, fearfully, longing to trust, yet deeply ambivalent. If she comes in despair and tears, it may feel terribly like surrender - for the moment. She knows she has high standards. Will you live up to them? She wants to have a perfect counsellor. She wants to be perfect in every way - and she wants to be the perfect client. These wishes cast a brittle, tense light across the first few sessions.

She knows she has dark and horrible secrets within her. That first phone call to make an appointment is so difficult - especially when she says 'I'm bulimic'. But at least now, you know about the eating behaviour. Perhaps she won't have to talk about the rest of it; how bad, deceitful, mean and nasty she is. How aggressive, sexual, unloving and unable she feels. All of this is obviously quite unacceptable. You, the counsellor, would never be like that.

Yet she expects, too, that you will be brisk with her, get on with the job, sort her out and force her to grow up, behave herself and stop messing up her life. She sort of wants this. She's used to being harsh with herself; what could be more reasonable than that you, the expert, should do it too? So it may be that your peaceable invitation to start exploring her inner world together takes her aback. The beginning of counselling for her can mean a rapid re-sorting of her ideas, and sometimes it's too hard to do; you aren't perfect, you don't 'sort her out' quickly, and furthermore it's just too much to contemplate revealing that part of her that's behind that inner wall. She leaves.

But for the client who stays, the work is painful, but sometimes intriguing and sometimes a relief. Things get easier as she realises that someone else knows about this. You don't think her disgusting; just your knowing about her life can make a difference.

The compulsively eating client

She has probably thought about coming into counselling for a long time, because she feels out of control. She's tried slimming clubs, doctors, the Cambridge diet; but it's all been a failure. She knows she's hopeless.

It's hard to justify using the time and money to try counselling - just another flop, probably (that's what her husband says). It's so self-indulgent, too, isn't it? She really has no right to someone else's attention and time - let alone care. There are lots of people in her world who deserve it more than she does. And really, she's quite used to not getting very much looking after. She can do without that sort of thing quite well.

Never mind. Now she's here, and really getting on very well with you. She gets on well with most people, after all. It's different in counselling, though; the focus on herself all the time can be uncomfortable. She's used to giving attention to other people and somehow you keep turning the light back on her. She keeps giving you little things to keep you happy - tells you she's feeling better already; has managed to circumvent a binge recently; how helpful she feels you are. What she has learned from her life experience is that you have to do your best, keep your end up in a relationship, don't ask for too much.

She can be the ideal 'compliant client'. It is very scary to expose some of the reality of her existence. That she is exhausted with giving all the time; that she wants some care too; that she's afraid that you, like everyone else in her life, will get fed up with her and withdraw your support. Especially if she doesn't work hard in counselling, and earn your care.

This tiring need to do what's expected may be a further drain on her, and lead her to wanting to leave counselling before things are really better. She can wrap all the mess up after a decent interval, smile bravely, and get the hell out of the counselling room before you latch on to what's really going on. It can be such a relief to her if you can catch this before it happens, and by your consistency and calmness, assure her that you are indeed willing to stay with her, listen to her long-buried pain, and see her as she really is.

At last she may begin to learn to forgive herself for needing food, care, love, rest. Later, she may even learn to appreciate her ability to get what she needs for herself. She doesn't have to remain deprived; she can find a balance for her life. She may learn to express her feelings directly, and nourish herself in all sorts of ways.

The anorexic client

Unlike the other two, the anorexic client may well come into counselling because someone else has pushed her into it. Her motivation for counselling is quite low. She knows, inside, that she's unhappy (but surely, once she's a little thinner everything will be all right?). Just possibly you might be able to help, but somehow she doubts it.

Will you make her eat, and make her fat? That's what everyone else seems to want her to do. And she won't put up with that, she simply can't tolerate it, it would be the destruction of all her fragile control over things. So she is guarded, careful. What she finds enormously reassuring is that you seem prepared to go very slowly and gently. When you say that you are aware that she isn't very well because she isn't eating enough to maintain her weight, she can take the time to see that it's so, because you don't seem prepared to try and rush her into taking more food.

So the perspective is long and the work slow. Sometimes she feels it's a waste of time. Her relatives are giving her a hard time, pushing her to eat, and she can talk with you about how to deal with that. You seem to feel she has rights! This is a new concept. Slowly, she begins to get the hang of taking her own decisions - both about her eating and body, and about her life. She faces the dilemmas over and over again. If she stands up for herself, will they hate her? If she emerges from her shell, will it be too dangerous to survive?

As she begins to feel safer, her eating changes. Sometimes this feels worse than before. She's losing control. She can't resist toffees, and chews them all the time; then she spits them out, horrified. She begins to binge behind closed doors, and hates herself for it. It's all made worse because if her family knew, they'd love it. Oh, wouldn't they crow! She's getting better, they'd laugh. Now we don't have to worry about her any more!

She may start to vomit, to get rid of the food she can no longer resist. This seems chaotic, unlike the pure, clean control of anorexia. It's messy, disgusting and shameful. She feels horribly fat. Instead of getting better, she's now got bulimia! There are times when she feels she could kill herself. But you seem quite calm about all this, and it's reassuring to know that some of the other people recovering from anorexia go through these feelings too. You seem confident that she will regain her balance around food eventually.

In the meantime, she is learning to be herself - an individual person. She learns that she is still loved, and that she can love herself, in spite of the growing and changing she is doing. She also learns that you will stay with her until she feels ready to go it alone.

Conclusion

It seems very hard that people in eating distress survey such a risky landscape when they seek help. There are indeed many excellent, caring and empathetic workers, who teach, write and practise, and to whom I owe my thanks. Whatever is good and useful in this guidebook has been gleaned from them. But there are others whose work is less aware, less scrupulous. These workers may brutalise and alienate the client; sadly, many counsellors meet clients who have been hurt, frightened and angered by going through such 'treatment', and helping clients to come to terms with what has happened to them is commonly part of the work we have to do together.

From the mid-70s, counselling people in eating distress developed alongside the feminist, gay and self-advocacy movements. People who had always been seen as the underdogs (women, psychiatric patients, gay people, fat people, etc.) began to gain a voice. We began to see that, far from being 'crazy', we were all part of the richness of life. We had a right to be here, exactly as we were. We could, after all, question the old monolithic orthodoxy.

I was a depressed compulsive eater in the 60s, before the new freedom began. I was given amphetamines, (to which I would have become addicted if I had been able to find an illegal supplier), stomach-fillers, and finally, an appointment with a psychiatrist. Weeping in his office, I was told that there was far more wrong with me than I realised. What, exactly, was mysteriously not specified. Weeks later, an impersonal appointment came through the post to attend an ongoing group - at the gothic psychiatric hospital twenty miles away (and me without a car), at a time when I would normally be working. I never went.

Years later, a self-help group, nurtured by the Women's therapy Centre, helped me to begin the long process of understanding and change which finally led me to health again. I have seen both sides of the help that was then available, and I know which I prefer.

I am open about this personal history because I want to take full responsibility for what I have written here. My mistakes are mine alone. I have learned a great deal from the wisdom and compassion of others, both those who wrote the books in the bibliography and less well-known workers. My own experience, I am sure, is exposed, for good or ill. I hope I have not been too prejudiced.

Writing a short booklet is a wonderful discipline, but at the end one longs to expand. In many sections, it has only been possible to flash headlines to the reader, when it would have been so much more satisfying to develop a topic into a book of its own. If you are working with people in eating distress, it is very nurturing to read widely, amongst the books of quality on the subject, and also in psychology, feminism, politics and so on. But of course, the way one really learns is through the extraordinary courage of one's clients.

Further Reading

Anorexia nervosa

Orbach, S: *Hunger Strike*. Faber & Faber, 1986.
Duker, M & Slade, R: *Anorexia Nervosa & Bulimia: How to Help*. Open University Press, 1988.
Bruch, H: *Eating Disorders: Obesity, Anorexia & the Person Within*. Routledge & Kegan Paul, 1974.
Bruch, H: *The Golden Gate*. Open Books, 1978.
MacLeod, S: *The Art of Starvation*. Virago, 1981.
Lawrence, M: *The Anorexic Experience*. Women's Press, 1984.

Bulimia nervosa

Roche, L: *Glutton for Punishment*. Pan Books, 1984.
Dana, M & Lawrence, M: *Women's Secret Disorder, A New Understanding of Bulimia*. Grafton Books, 1988.

Compulsive eating

Orbach, S: *Fat is a Feminist Issue*. Hamlyn, 1978.
Orbach, S: *Fat is a Feminist Issue 2*. Arrow, 1988.
Roberts, R: *Breaking All the Rules*. Viking, 1985.
Roth, G: *Feeding the Hungry Heart*. Grafton Books, 1986.
Roth, G: *When Food is Love* Grafton Books, 1992.

General reading

Norwood, R: *Women Who Love Too Much* Arrow Books, 1988.
Chernin, K: *Womansize, the Tyranny of Slenderness*. Women's Press, 1981.
Chernin, K: *The Hungry Self, Women, Eating & Identity*. Virago, 1986.
Lawrence, M: *Fed Up & Hungry, Women, Oppression & Food*. Women's Press, 1987.
Black, C: *It Will Never Happen To Me*. (Adult children of alcoholics). Ballantine Books, New York, 1981.
Bass, E & Davis, L: *The Courage to Heal: A Guide for Women Survivors of Child Sexual Abuse*. Harper & Row, New York, 1988.
McCormick, E: Nervous Breakdown: *A Positive Guide to Coping, Healing & Rebuilding*. Unwin Paperbacks, 1988.